Yanking Bootstraps

Tammy Hawk-Bridges

> Dear Mick
> I wish you the greatest of success in your new business.
> Love,
> Tammy

Copyright © 2013 Tammy Hawk-Bridges

All rights reserved. No part of this book may be reproduced in any form without written permission by the author, with the exception of brief quotations for review.

Editor: Kelli Dugan

ISBN-13: 978-0615756288
ISBN-10: 061575628X

To My Honey,

Thank you for believing in me.

CONTENTS

Author's Letter *1*

Preface *3*

Chapter 1 **Do Your Research!** *9*

Chapter 2 **When Can I Quit My Job?** *12*

Chapter 3 **Cash is King** *15*

Chapter 4 **The Fear** *17*

Chapter 5 **Take Care of Yourself** *20*

Chapter 6 **Evaluate Relationships** *23*

Chapter 7 **Get a Coach** *26*

Chapter 8 **Learn to Sell** *29*

Chapter 9 **Treating Myself Like an Employee** *32*

Chapter 10 **Building Your Pipeline** *35*

Chapter 11 **Pick a Lane** *38*

Chapter 12 **Marketing/Finding Your Perfect Equation** *41*

Chapter 13 **Stay the Course** *47*

Chapter 14 **Take Action!** *51*

Chapter 15 **Your Pricing Strategy** *54*

Chapter 16 **The Crazies/Turning Down Bad Business** *57*

Chapter 17 **Ignorance is NOT Bliss** *60*

Chapter 18 **Branding** *64*

CONTENTS

Chapter 19 **The REAL Cost of Doing Business With Your Friends** *67*

Chapter 20 **The Middle Part** *70*

Chapter 21 **Discovering the Law of Attraction** *73*

Chapter 22 **Rotten Milk** *77*

Chapter 23 **Ten of My Biggest Mistakes** *80*

Guest Authors *85*

About the Author *89*

"When it is dark enough,

you can see the stars."

Ralph Waldo Emerson

A Labor of Love

If you are a struggling entrepreneur trying to find your way, this book was written from my heart especially for you. And even if you aren't starting a business for the first time on a hope and a prayer, you will also find valuable insight as well.

In the past three and a half years I have had three businesses: the first one failed; the second one, although successful, I found wasn't my purpose; and the third – well, we'll see, but it looks *very* promising! Ironically, the most valuable lessons learned were from failure, reminding me of a favorite Thomas Edison quote: *"I have not failed. I've just found 10,000 ways that won't work."*

I can't think of enough adjectives to describe how tough the beginning of this journey was. The first year on my own was one of the hardest things I've ever endured, and I'm not just speaking of going through the steps of starting up a business from nothing. I'm also talking about recovering from being broken.

I'd lost my confidence, and I was questioning who I was.

In the beginning, every day was a struggle to persevere. There were times when all I wanted to do was lie in bed and say, "Screw it!" However, that little pulling feeling in my gut always managed to show up just at the right time and put my feet on the floor.

"Yanking Bootstraps" is laid out to set the stage within the preface and then cover a specific topic in each chapter. The chapters are brief, straight to the point and valuable. The book was laid out with the intention that you could read it in a weekend and make some changes in your business that following Monday.

For a few of the chapters you will find commentary from a guest writer. The entrepreneurs asked to participate in this project were very carefully selected. They are my heroes and the influences inspiring me to push myself to the next level. They are extraordinary business leaders who are truly passionate not only about their own success but for that of others. I am so thrilled, excited, and appreciative to have them as a part of this project! A very heart-felt thank you to all of you!

I want to give a very special thank you to my editor, Kelli Dugan: This book isn't possible without you! Thank you for putting up with me. I know it was no easy task.

Last but not least, thank you to my wonderful husband, Kirt, for believing in me even when you didn't understand.

With Love,
Tammy

Preface

Striking out on your own is certainly not for the weak-hearted, and sadly that's why so many great ideas go unexplored.

In three years I've gone from primary breadwinner to small business owner to small business failure to small business strategist and business mentor. This book was written to share with you everything I wish someone could have told me at the beginning of my journey.

If there is one thing I know about myself beyond a shadow of doubt, it's that I was born an entrepreneur, but that hasn't always necessarily meant I had to literally own a business. For me, being an entrepreneur is a mindset. It's the acceptance of great responsibility, the willingness to work as hard as it takes, and a very passionate need to feel a sense of ownership.

In every position I have held in my career, it was crucial for me to have a sense of independence. In that freedom I was capable of excellence and my entrepreneurial needs were met. I would treat my position like it was my own business, and that mindset has made me very successful in every job I've ever held.

However, when subjected to leadership that was more of a dictatorship, I wilted like a flower without water. Micromanaging suppresses my creativity, and as my drive for excellence dwindles, I know it's time to look for a new challenge.

I've always had a tremendous work ethic, which has always been a huge part of who I am. When I reached a point in my life where this was belittled, it was devastating. It created a sense of insecurity that rocked me at my core. I'd spent several years working in a career that I loved. It meant something to me, and I had many accomplishments to show for it.

In an instant – and with the decision of one person – it was reduced to meaning nothing. I felt mocked, insignificant, and irrelevant. I had reached a breaking point. In that moment I made a decision that I would never put myself in a position where this could ever happen to me again.

Perhaps I should be thankful? It was this experience that gave me the courage to go out on my own. But the question remains: Can I do this entrepreneur thing for real?

Can a hobby be a viable business?
I've always loved photos and have had a fascination with them for years. I don't have many photos from my childhood, and as I got older, the lack of tangible memories created a void. I wanted to make sure my own children didn't share this fate, so I constantly tortured them with my camera. They certainly didn't appreciate my motives at the time, but I know that someday they will.

I grew bored with just taking pictures and putting them into my photo albums and was always looking for something more artistic to do with them. I'd purchased a printer that came with some filters that added dynamic characteristics to my photos and loved exploring that. However, being the overly ambitious person that I am, this didn't challenge me for very long. I purchased Photoshop and a book of tutorials and was on my way to being a graphic artist, intoxicated by the possibilities.

I am a huge Andy Warhol fan, so I enjoyed duplicating some of his work with my own family's portraits. After countless nights in front of the computer, I learned to do lots of interesting designs. I then lined up a printer to put my designs to canvas and a framer to complete the piece. It was coming together, and the end result was beautiful.

In the beginning this was just something to do for myself, family and friends, but as time went on, I dreamed of doing it professionally.

At the realization of my soon-coming corporate demise, I started to quickly structure my hobby as a business. I lined up suppliers, designed a website, and PhotoCandy was born. After eight months of planning, I was ready to quit my "real" job.

I gave PhotoCandy all my effort, armed with the knowledge and expertise I had at that time. I gave it a year, working sometimes 18-hour days – seven days a week. I often felt like a mad scientist, literally shutting myself off from my family and the world for hours and sometimes days. I tried to create a business that would give me financial freedom and a permanent get-out-of-corporate-America pass.

It took me about six months to realize there were some holes in my plan. It just wasn't happening, and I certainly couldn't see how this business was going to support my family. We were barely out of the recession – depending on whom you asked – and it was hard to sell products that were a want versus a need. I was under the very naive impression that if I worked my ass off and gave it 150 percent that I could NOT fail. I was so incredibly wrong.

Admitting defeat, sort of

I was exhausted mentally and physically, but as someone that equates quitting to failure, I continued on way too long. One night after a long few days of working practically nonstop I climbed into bed early with a copy of *Success* magazine. I flipped through the articles and came across one that was about how important it was that post–recession entrepreneurs made sure their businesses were needs based.

I read one line over and over: "If it doesn't make cents, it doesn't make sense," and with tears rolling down my face I admitted that PhotoCandy was over.

Then something hit me.

I sprang from the bed and ran upstairs to my office. I'd learned how to use Facebook for my business, and I realized it was the only tool generating any business at all for me. I'd even learned to capture sales through the social networking site and how to use all sorts of cool applications that literally turned my page into a very impressive web-like presence.

As a marketing person it hit me that companies were coming to Facebook in droves but leaving their branding behind. This is where companies are social! It's like showing up to the black-tie party in your torn up jeans. It seemed they didn't know they could brand their companies this way using social platforms.

I saw my opportunity and pounced!

I'd take the same graphic design skills I used in PhotoCandy and I will teach myself all the complicated specifics. Then I will use this skill to teach businesses how to create a smashing social media presence that incorporated their brand!

Just as the sun began to rise, I had a new business venture.

A failure can breed success
The biggest problem when I started SocialHeavy was my financial situation. PhotoCandy had drained my financial resources. I literally had NOTHING left.

Did I have regrets for spending everything I had to create a business that couldn't make it? Absolutely not! How could I? It was building PhotoCandy that gave me the idea for SocialHeavy, the business that would guide me to my purpose.

In the beginning, having my own business had one goal: To keep me the hell out of corporate America. However as time moved on, I learned new things, got exposed to different types of people, and realized my *true* passion.

Trusting your instincts

I ended PhotoCandy without wasting any time wound licking. I leveraged my skills to develop a business in the fast-growing social media realm. In developing SocialHeavy I covered every base missed with the failed business. In addition I studied everything I could get my hands on in regards to marketing and growing a profitable business. It paid off; I was able to make my new business profitable very quickly.

I enjoyed building SocialHeavy, and really thought it was my final destination. I developed the business because I knew the services I offered were in demand.

For some reason, though, the yearning – *pulling* – feeling that was with me from day one still didn't feel content. Over time, while working with my clients I learned they were attracted to me for more than my graphic design skills. They were attracted to my perspectives on growing a small business and my knack for marketing.

I learned that most entrepreneurs didn't have basic marketing knowledge; they didn't know how to expand their business; and what's more, they didn't have a plan in general. In addition, they were not prepared to deal with all the changes that technology was bringing. The most heart-breaking observation was watching them repeat the very mistakes I'd made that caused my failure. The path I was meant for revealed itself – finally, after almost four years.

It was then I combined all the marketing knowledge I had learned to make SocialHeavy a quick success. I created a business plan to launch the Perfect Marketing Equation. The Perfect Marketing Equation is a step-by-step system designed to teach entrepreneurs: (1) how to build a solid foundation for a business and (2) how to design a practical marketing strategy specific to their needs and business model.

Sometimes you don't have all the answers. You just trust that in time they will reveal themselves, and you *cannot* afford to stand still while you wait. Keep moving toward your goals even if you aren't 100 percent certain they're on target.

Most importantly, never be afraid to fail. Every failure and success is necessary because that knowledge and experience inches you closer to your true calling.

Transforming failure into inspiration

Loneliness was the only thing rivaling my fear that first year, but it drove me to write this book. I want to bring comfort to the person starting a business with nothing more than a dream, hope and a prayer. It can be done!

It's okay to be afraid! Hell, it's even necessary. Fear actually motivated me. Honestly, I'd wonder about you if you weren't afraid.

In a nutshell, I left my job and started a business with close to zero resources. And keep in mind, I hadn't been working for shoe money but had been the primary breadwinner in my family. Failure was not an option for me.

Unfortunately, I did things the hard way, and I made lots of mistakes. I'm thankful for some of those missteps because they were an essential part of growth and learning, but they can also cost a lot of money and heartache.

This book is intended to give you real, no-nonsense advice drawn from my own experiences. I assure you the information included in these chapters can be implemented right away and will create a significant impact on your business.

I hope this book inspires, comforts and informs you, but my primary objective is to encourage you to put a solid marketing framework in place that will eliminate your fear, so you can grow a profitable business.

CHAPTER ONE

Do Your Research!

One of the most crucial beginnings of a business is determining whether or not you have a valid idea and if it's going to be profitable enough to sustain you.

With PhotoCandy, I had a beautiful product, a decent head for business, and a great talent for sales. How could I lose, right?

Wrong!

There were so many factors I didn't take into account. I had researched my competitors pretty well, so I knew what I was up against. However, back then I didn't know anything about email marketing, search engine optimization, or Google ad words to create web traffic.

Facebook was the only marketing medium I was using to reach people, and that alone just wasn't enough. I also didn't take into account that I had a product dependent on customer participation, and we live in an instant gratification culture. People tend to procrastinate when they see something is going to cost them time.

Bottom line, I didn't evaluate my opportunities sufficiently with PhotoCandy, and that was a huge mistake.

By contrast. when I started SocialHeavy, I drew from that experience, and I was very careful about the business model I was creating. In choosing my target market, for example, I took a long, hard look at my potential demographics.

Who was I going to sell to? My primary product at that time was social media branding. Companies in my neck of the woods at that time were intrigued by social media but not really onboard with actually implementing it into their marketing strategies. I realized quickly that selling my product must first be an educational process–something I didn't have time for.

I needed to make sales quickly, so I positioned SocialHeavy as a virtual, Internet-based company. I started out calling on larger markets that had already embraced social media and understood without too much coaxing the value of branding themselves in that space.

It's one thing to create a side business where the goal is just to make a little extra money. Mistakes are rarely fatal. Sure, you may lose some money, but if your primary source of income remains intact, you won't lose your house.

In my case – as the primary breadwinner – there was no room for error. Not this time around. With SocialHeavy, it was literally sink or swim like hell. I had to be very careful, and I had to have some really good answers to some tough questions.

"Have you done the REAL math?"

Until you answer these questions, you're wasting your time:

1. How big is the market for this product or service? If you're going to serve a niche or target, is it large enough to sustain your business?

2. Is your product a hard or easy sell? What I mean by that is will you have to educate your clients before they buy? *It's key to know if your product involves a long sales cycle — meaning clients will not be able to decide in that hot second to buy — because you will need to plan adequately for long periods in between sales. This also means you'll need a larger pipeline and to be more aggressive in your sales efforts. The more costly the product, the harder you'll have to work at selling it.*

3. How hard will your target market be to reach? What will be your plan for reaching them? How much will it cost?

4. Who is doing this already? Do they seem to be successful at it? Could you potentially compete with them? What is their price point? How does it compare to yours? *By the way, don't get too excited when you see that nobody is doing something. There might be a reason, so proceed cautiously.*

5. Does your product cost a lot to produce? Are the materials plentiful? Are you going to be able to charge enough to make a *profit? Profit, by the way, is the amount left over once you pay for ALL expenses.*

Do you have a business plan? Doing this exercise is essential to asking some deep questions. If I had done this exercise in round one of my business, it would have saved me a lot of money and heartache. Check out *The One Page Business Plan* by Jim Horan, it's an easy exercise that will help you answer some hard questions.

CHAPTER TWO

When Can I Quit My Job?

This is the scary part: Giving up the known for the unknown.

Knowing when to quit your job actually depends on you and the type of business you want to start. Some types of businesses can be managed quite easily while working full time, while others demand your full attention.

Something that's just as important to consider as the "money factor" is asking a simple question: Is being an entrepreneur the right thing for *you*? It can be an extremely rewarding experience to be in charge of your own destiny and start living a life with no limitations! However, it can also be very stressful, and you have to be *very* truthful with yourself.

Are you the right person for this? Are you willing to work extremely hard, harder than you've ever worked in your life? Are you willing to work late into the night and on weekends? Are you willing to do things that are outside of your comfort zone such as selling? Are you self-motivated? Are you good with money?

You will need to be extremely self-motivated and able to pull yourself through the many disappointments. Most importantly, you'll have to learn to be very disciplined and cut back on things you don't need.

However, you will also need to be smart enough to know when you do need to invest money into your business in order to create growth.

Above all, be certain you're choosing entrepreneurship for the right reasons. Hating your present job or feeling stifled are simply not strong enough motivators to carry you through the frustration and seemingly endless hassles that plague every startup.

Quitting your job will definitely free you from that employer you hate, but don't fool yourself: Working harder than you've ever worked in your life will hardly feel like freedom. Believing wholeheartedly in your business and yourself can open doors you never dreamed possible – especially when you're willing to do *whatever* it takes – but there's really only one reason to take that leap and strike out on your own. Choose entrepreneurship because you have a great idea that fills a need in an underserved market.

"Are you ready to step WAY outside your comfort zone?"

Your business will never survive – much less thrive – without a strong support system. Make sure the people in your life understand the risk you're taking, and that it won't always be smiles and sunshine. And remember, any setbacks your business experiences affect your significant other and can breed resentment, so tread carefully if that support is lacking.

Before you even *consider* quitting your job, however, make certain you surround yourself with other successful entrepreneurs, and learn from their mistakes before *you* make them. Don't believe for a second you can do this all by yourself. You'll need their guidance and expertise, especially when it comes to what-not-to-do. When I left the cubicle nation, I had three months of expenses in the bank. Guess what? It wasn't nearly enough, and I cut things way too close.

I did fund my business mainly with cash, which is something I highly recommend. There are times when it may be okay to use debt, and we will talk about this later on. However, you do not want to go into debt over a business that you haven't even started yet and have no idea if it is going to work or not.

Try to go six months without spending your paychecks. Pay your bills and live on the money that your business makes only. When you can do that for that period of time, chances are you are going to be okay. Even so, you are going to have to be very careful with your money.

I have known many people that started a business while working full time. It is possible, and unless you have a large amount of capital available to you, I highly recommend this approach. If you're truly passionate about your business idea, you'll do whatever it takes. Even if that means working 18 hours a day to get it off the ground before you quit your job. That's exactly what I did.

However, all that being said, there does come a time when you will need to "*burn the lifeboat*". When you have all the right things in place and you *know* that you have a profitable idea, you must go for it. The reason I say this is from the experience of working with entrepreneurs, they typically need *a motivator*. Meaning they need a fire under their ass to start moving forward. It's amazing what you'll do when you have to, and failure isn't an option. Long story short, most people don't make their business endeavors work, unless they really have to. *Fear is a great motivator.*

Expert Insight: Barbara Corcoran
Real estate and business expert, bestselling author, "Shark" investor on ABC's Shark Tank.

"There will never be an ideal time to quit your job. The best advice I can give you is to take a leap of faith. Convince yourself that you deserve to have a successful business and you are capable of making it happen. If you have a good idea, and you think the opportunity is there, just jump! Jump off the cliff without logic. If you jump off the cliff and put yourself in that position, you will figure it out on the way down!"

CHAPTER THREE

Cash is King

SocialHeavy wasn't my first rodeo. I actually left my job to start another business, but it didn't work out.

The problem? I'd already gone through all of my resources with the first business. I'm not ashamed to say that I had no money left in the bank. It was sink or swim. I flipped from one business to another, and out of fear of losing my house, I made it work.

Cash flow is the single most important factor in any successful business. According to the U.S Small Business Administration, more than 50 percent of small businesses fail in the first five years, and insufficient capital is the leading culprit.

I've seen many people geek out on an "entrepreneurial high" and go rent the fancy loft office before they close their first deal. I've often heard the explanation, "Well, for people to take me seriously, I have to look like a real business." That's an absolute load of crap and just an excuse for a really bad decision. It's very normal in this day and time to run a business and sleep under the same roof!

It's simple economics. It's extremely hard to get a small business bank loan in a post-recession economy. The most common alternatives are a home equity loan, getting an angel investor (also no easy task), borrowing from a family member or using a credit card.

The world turns on credit. People borrow to do the things that they couldn't normally do, and there are times when it's warranted. But I've also known people who start businesses entirely on credit, taking out second mortgages on their homes and maxing out their credit cards. Be smarter than that.

I suggest not borrowing money or using credit until you've completed your business plan, established you have a valid business idea that is profitable, and you're already making sales.

Let's say you've done all three of these things, and now you need a website. Your cash is tapped, but you have a credit card. Go ahead and charge it. At that point you're investing in something that has been proven to be worthy. Certain things are going to be necessary for you to take your business where it needs to go. Website? Yes. Fancy office furniture so you feel like a "real" business? That's a big fat NO!

A strategically used credit card can certainly provide a temporary loan to help grow your business, but you need to determine if an investment will make money and how long it will take. Make sure you set a budget for the things you don't have cash for, and stick to it. If you have a credit card that you have used for a couple of big purchases for your business, it's always a good idea to put that card aside and pay it down as soon as possible.

CHAPTER FOUR

The Fear

I have a love-hate relationship with fear. Fear can be completely evil and totally rule us if we let it. However, fear is necessary because it can help keep you grounded and in check. It can actually put your feet on the floor in the mornings when you are discouraged and tired.

I'll be honest. I've had my fair share of days when I just wanted to lie in bed and say screw it. There have been days that I *did* stay in bed, with the covers pulled over my head, so afraid that I literally trembled.

I want you to know that it's okay to be afraid. Early on, before I had a business coach, I wish I had someone in my life that could have just said those words to me. It would have meant everything!

"It's okay to be afraid."

Why wouldn't you be afraid? Uncertainty is terrifying! Risking everything we own, letting down our families, going without medical benefits, just not knowing what is going to happen, or if we're going to be able to pay our bills.

It is so easy to become consumed in our business in the beginning out of fear of failing, especially when our success or failure impacts others like our family. The flipside is fear can push you to succeed; it can push you outside your comfort zone into greatness.

Where I went wrong in the beginning was I let fear rule my existence to the point that I blocked everything and everyone else out of my life and just focused on the business. I didn't communicate with my husband. I ignored my kids. I turned down opportunities to go out to dinner with my friends. Hell, there were times I would go days without going outside. It wasn't healthy, and we'll talk more about this in the next chapter!

I promise you that fear is necessary to feel, especially in the beginning. However, I also promise you that as time goes on, the feeling will be less intense. I think that in being an entrepreneur you are always going to have some element of fear to deal with. I know for me I am a risk-taker by nature, and whenever you take risks, there is a natural element of fear. A risk without fear would be no risk at all.

There are ways to overcome the fear, though, and I have learned them all the hard way.

1. **There is great comfort in having a plan.** Don't spend your day worrying about how you are going to get customers and pay your bills. You must have a marketing framework to operate in and if you don't have one – get one ASAP! You should never rely on "being motivated" in your business. Let's face it, we are not always motivated. Design a framework or a plan, stay focused, and plow through.

2. **Pursue greatness and subject yourself to it as often as possible!** Surround yourself with entrepreneurs who understand your struggles. Seek out people that are positive, strong, smarter than you, and achieve connections with them. I have found authors and speakers that inspire me, and I keep their videos and books close by for when I need a little jolt. Avoid negative and needy people like the plague!

3. **Accept hardship.** Know in advance that starting a business will be one of the hardest things you ever do. Mentally prepare yourself for this in the very beginning. Tell yourself that you *will* have bad weeks, so bad that you will want to

quit. You *will* be afraid that you are going to fail. This is normal and it *WILL* pass as long as you are doing the things you are supposed to do.

I absolutely love this quote by Dale Carnegie and it is so true!

"Inaction breeds doubt and fear. Action breeds confidence and courage. If you want to conquer fear, do not sit home and think about it. Go out and get busy."

Expert Insight: Dr. Shannon Reese
Sport psychologist, peak performance expert, and business coach

"What is fear? A common acronym is False Evidence Appearing Real. The truth is that much of your fear is imagined, therefore, created by you. Your internal warning system is designed to help you navigate real fear, preventing you from physical or emotional harm. But a great majority of your fear falls under the imagined category and is a product of your mind working overtime to make sense of the unknowns of a new situation. As intense as real fear, imagined fear can hold you back from reaching your potential in business and life. The great news is that you can turn your fear from a liability into an asset by taking the time to understand it. Fear can be used as an effective tool to open your eyes to opportunities or alternatives that you might have otherwise overlooked. It can also increase your awareness of obstacles you must face and areas where you need to grow. Understanding and befriending the "enemy" that lives within is the first step toward your business success."

CHAPTER FIVE

Take Care of Yourself

One of the biggest mistakes I made when I started my business was not taking proper care of myself. Women by nature put themselves last because we are accustomed to taking care of everyone else. Well, I wasn't last. I wasn't at all.

I was in the throes of starting a business, and I was terrified I wasn't going to be able to make it work or pay my bills.

I'd go days without leaving my house, and this behavior didn't go unpunished. I developed a chronic and painful circulatory problem from sitting in front of the computer for hours on end. Even more depressing, I put on 25 pounds from sleep deprivation and lack of exercise. Funny thing was, I hardly ever ate. I also learned during a routine medical exam I'd acquired a vitamin D deficiency from lack of sunlight.

I finally said, "Okay, that's it!"

I don't know about you, but I'm over forty, so my body is not so forgiving anymore. What I do to my body not only shows in how I look, but more importantly, how I feel.

I became incredibly depressed at one point. I know for a fact it was self-inflicted because I wasn't allowing myself rest and enjoyment. As I look back now, I believe with all my heart I was punishing myself. I didn't feel that I deserved to have fun and laugh. I was putting my family's well being in jeopardy.

I finally gave myself permission to take a mental break, even if the house payment was due in two weeks, and I had no idea how I was going to pay it! I learned the hard way that when I took time to go outside, acknowledge the earth and breath the air that my perspective changed. I felt more energized and the depression lifted. And guess what happened? With my head clear, I was more creative and productive!

I know, for example, how easy it is to be so involved in your work that you miss lunch. I actually have made a routine now. Every day, at the same time, I leave my work for at least 30 minutes to an hour. I have some lunch, watch my favorite cooking show or take a walk. It gives me the mental break I need, and then I am right back to work.

It is imperative that you exercise, eat healthy, and relax your mind and spirit. Trust me, it will make a difference!

"Sometimes you just have to say, screw it!"

So go outside and smell the breeze! Go to the bookstore and relax with a good book *(that is not about business!!)* and a cup of coffee. Go to lunch with your friends! Hell, go see a movie in the middle of the day! Enjoy some of the perks of working for yourself! Just on occasion I want you to say, *"Screw it!"* If you don't, what's it all for anyway?

Expert Insight: Eliz Greene

Author, professional speaker, and national spokesperson for the American Heart Association

"Set your timer to be healthy and productive at your desk!"

"One of the best productivity tips I ever received was to break up the day into small segments and focus on a particular task. This strategy works well to keep you healthy at the same time."

"First, set your timer for 15 or 20 minutes and then focus on work. When the timer goes off, stop and spend 20 seconds in a body position opposite of the one you were just in."

For example, if you are at your computer typing away:

- Stop and sit up straight.
- Stretch your arms to the sides.
- Squeeze your shoulder blades together.
- Push your chest open.

"This allows the muscle to reset and relax. You'll find yourself less fatigued at the end of the day. Have a drink of water, reset your timer and focus on the next task."

"After 3 rounds - or once per hour - stand up!"

"Spend 3 to 5 minutes on your feet. Walk over and refill your water glass or bottle. You need about 64 ounces of water per day. Drinking about 8 ounces every hour can make it easy to stay hydrated."

"Taking time out to take care of yourself can make a big difference in how you feel at the end of the day."

CHAPTER SIX

Evaluate Relationships

Remember the high school cafeteria? The teachers had their table, and so did the popular kids, the jocks, the outcasts (my table), the kids with uncertain sexual orientation, and so on.

Then, I found that behavior stupid. Now, I understand that hierarchy reflects a very natural human need to be in the presence of others similar to ourselves. It keeps us from feeling lonely and isolated in the world, and I was very lonely when my small business journey began.

Having the entrepreneur bug is not something everyone understands. My husband didn't understand it, and God love him, he tried so hard. Don't get me wrong, he was absolutely wonderful to me, but he's only ever worked for someone else his entire life.

He didn't understand me putting myself through the wringer, much less doing it on purpose. Sure, he took on household responsibilities, became the house cook for an entire year and exhibited a ton of empathy for how hard I worked. But empathy wasn't what I needed. What I really needed was someone to understand how gut-wrenchingly awful all this made me feel and yet get why I chose to do it anyway.

I finally realized one thing never changes no matter how old we get: People we spend time with impact our lives. Their opinions, lifestyles, and choices affect the decisions we make and shapes the people we become, and that is absolutely crucial to our success.

A strong and positive mindset is a must-have for any successful entrepreneur. Striking out on your own takes a tremendous amount of courage and confidence. We must believe in ourselves and our ability to make it happen. If you have someone around you that is polluting your mindset, it will make your mission much more difficult, if not impossible.

A critical first step in my entrepreneurial journey was to evaluate my relationships. There were – as my husband calls them –Downer Debbies in my life. Downer Debbies are negative and typically everything about them is. They rarely take interest in your life because they'd rather keep the focus on what's wrong in theirs – which is almost always everything. They are to be avoided at all costs, especially when your business is in its infancy, because they will zap every ounce of energy you should be devoting to your baby.

> *"You need people who are smarter than you."*

What you *will* need are people who understand firsthand the challenges and pressures you face as a startup and who are quick to offer advice and support. It is very important to have people that are on equal ground with you, but it is even more important to have people in your life that make you reach for something more. Simply put, you will always be more successful in the presence of successful people.

You *need* people in your life who are smarter than you, more successful than you, and who make you *want* to be better. I know too many people who reject others who make them feel inferior, but without these mentors and role models in our lives, we will never see we *can* be better.

Expert Insight: Natalie MacNeil

Creator of SheTakesOnTheWorld.com and bestselling author of "She Takes on the World: A Guide to Being Your Own Boss, Working Happy, and Living on Purpose"

"I have come to realize that the people you choose to surround yourself with is the most important decision you make day-to-day. Surround yourself with people who raise you up, not those who try to bring you down. I have ended relationships with people close to me because of the negative energy they were constantly bringing into my life. That may sound harsh, but I would do it again. If you want to be your best, you have to surround yourself with the best people you can."

CHAPTER SEVEN

Get a Coach

A coach is a successful entrepreneur's secret weapon, and I'm not talking about a handbag! It's imperative that you share only a business relationship with this person, though, so you absolutely cannot ask your friend, spouse, pastor or favorite uncle to do the deed.

You might say, "But I don't need a coach." You're wrong. I'm extremely disciplined and structured; yet I still need a business coach. I think it's also necessary to say that some of the greatest business leaders I know all confess to having coaches. It's especially necessary when you're new to the trenches, scared to death, and feeling lost.

I could probably list 100 benefits of having a business coach, but here is my Top 8:

1. **Perspective**. There is tremendous value in having a different perspective than your own, especially when it's unbiased and experienced.

2. **Accountability**. No more putting things on your list that you never get done. Plan and implement.

3. **Feedback**. You now have someone who can help you make tough decisions. Bounce ideas off your coach, and he or she won't just tell you what you want to hear.

4. **Partnership**. Having a business coach will help you feel like you have someone in the fire pit with you when times are tough.

5. **Strategy**. Coaches help devise a strategic action plan that prevents you from contracting the "I-don't-know-what-to-do blues" or the more dreaded Shiny Object Syndrome. (If you don't know what the Shiny Object Syndrome is, please see Chapter 23: Ten of My Biggest Mistakes.)

6. **Goals**. One of the hardest things to do alone in your business is setting financial goals and then having the discipline to follow through. A coach will keep you on task.

7. **Money**. It may seem scary to invest in paying a business coach, but a good one can save you from making costly mistakes.

8. **Time**. Having a great business coach who made it through the entrepreneurial maze and came out on the other side means having guidance, support and expertise at your disposal and possibly trimming the start-up phase from years to months.

Like any relationship, it's also important you have certain chemistry with your coach. When interviewing a potential coach be painfully honest about your weaknesses, strengths and needs, so you find the right fit. Most will offer a free consultation to become acquainted and see if you feel like you can connect with them. And *always* ask for references.

Expert Insight: Nik Lemmens
Author and licensed career coach

"Even coaches get coaches. Yes, that's right. I'm a business and career coach, and I work with a coach, too. But a coach is only effective when they can make you take action, either in a new direction or an improvement on what you're already doing. What's the point of setting goals if you aren't taking action to achieve them?"

"A good coach will listen and question a lot, so they can make you realize what you can improve and help you "buy in" to possible solutions. Don't confuse this with consultants who come in, look at data, ask questions and provide you with *their* solution. A coach will encourage you to find your own solution."

CHAPTER EIGHT

Learn to Sell

I was shocked to learn how few small business owners really know how to sell their own product.

People are generally okay with going to networking events and posting on Facebook. However, they are a little more skittish about calling someone up they haven't been properly introduced to and asking them for an opportunity to talk to them about their business.

In my personal experience, business owners are generally very *passive* when it comes to sales. I am here to tell you that if you become more of a proactive salesperson, and develop a more strategic effort, your business will flourish at a more accelerated pace. I personally guarantee it!

> *"You're going to have to learn how to sell."*

Getting your message out is going to involve numerous platforms such as having a website, networking, doing email marketing, social media and blogging. When used correctly, these are all great marketing tools that can grow your business over time. If you want to jump start the process, however, you *must* be more proactive. You have to move out of your comfort zone to set things into motion.

You need to put yourself out there and ask people to buy your product. The most important thing to remember when you're talking to someone about your business is to be sincere and passionate. You must *believe* that you are doing an amazing thing by providing a product or service that's either going to fulfill a need or solve a problem.

I suggest you read some of my favorite works on the art of salesmanship, including Jeffrey Gitomer's *"Little Red Book of Selling"* and the must-read *"The Complete Idiot's Guide to Cold Calling"* by Keith Rosen." I am also a HUGE Zig Ziglar fan, his books made me an award-winning salesperson, and his *"Secrets of Closing the Sale"* has no equal.

Trust me when I say that not many people have this talent, and these tools will put you leaps ahead of the crowd. Over the next few chapters you will learn the necessary steps to create a sales strategy for your business that will get results!

Expert Insight: Alice Heiman
Nationally recognized sales expert, professional speaker, author

Nobody Told Me I Would Have To Sell!

"There are so many hats you must wear as an entrepreneur and so many things that will fill up your time, but if you don't learn to sell and make time to do it, your business won't succeed. Most people resist selling because they think of it as having to talk someone into buying something they don't need or want. That's coercion, not selling."

"Selling is problem solving. Selling is learning to ask your prospects good questions and listening to the answers, so you can help them find solutions. To be successful in sales you have to believe in yourself, believe in your product and believe you can help your customer. Sure, there are lots of sales skills you can learn that will help you succeed, but first you have to get out there and converse with people who can use your solution and find out the best way to help them do that. Then they will buy, and your business will be a success."

CHAPTER NINE

Treat Yourself Like an Employee

We've all seen those multi-level marketing ads, offering the freedom of business ownership and wealth in exchange for just a few hours of work per week. I distinctly remember one that said something like, "Make $20,000 per month and just work a few minutes a day!" I know what those ads cost, so someone must be falling for it.

Who *doesn't* want the freedom of being boss-free and wealthy with hardly any work involved? The problem is it's not a realistic goal. If you go into your venture believing that scenario is possible, you're going to be more than disappointed.

Startup entrepreneurs work ridiculous hours and often earn less than minimum wage after they do the *real math*. I certainly did in the beginning. And although we have no boss to report to every day, we still answer to clients, so is there really a difference?

Yes! The difference is HUGE! It's called *ownership*. I don't mind the endless hours of work, as long as I'm doing something I love that *belongs to me.*

You have to be disciplined enough to set challenging goals for yourself, though. It forces you to think through what you need for your business to be profitable and gives you a framework within which to work.

In the beginning, I struggled so hard to figure out how to make enough money to hang on to my business and continue. I would've done just about anything to prevent returning to corporate America. It's amazing how much time you spend just spinning your wheels, being afraid, and pacing the floor. If only I had a dollar for every sleepless night I walked the floor, and then came my "ah-ha" moment.

In my corporate career I'd been a professional, award-winning sales executive. I knew exactly what it took to bring in the sales needed to keep a business alive. But you know what? I wasn't doing any of it!

I was too busy being *self-employed*. Yeah, I was working 12- to 18-hour days, but I wasn't working smart, and I wasn't working within a structured plan. The things that had made me a very successful salesperson had been a strategically built and meticulously maintained database; a consistent, daily effort dedicated to business development and marketing; and most importantly, FOLLOWING UP.

I decided that if my business was going to survive, I had to start treating myself like an employee. It was time to put a very stern structure in place, stop pacing and start thinking strategically.

"Be disciplined enough to set goals and follow through."

As a salesperson I had goals, very aggressive goals that I had to work hard to achieve. That's what I was missing! I knew that drive was key to succeeding, so why hadn't it occurred to me to implement sales goals for myself? Perhaps I related this structure to the life I was so desperately trying to escape? Either way, it didn't matter: If I didn't get it together fast, I was going to fail at yet another business.

The difference between my corporate sales career and now is that I'm setting these goals for *myself*. One of the hardest things you'll face as an entrepreneur is having the discipline to hold your own feet to the fire. Unlike setting unrealistic and even unattainable goals that were set for me by past bosses, I can now set achievable goals based on *my own needs*. The trick, however, is setting aggressive enough goals you feel challenged without setting yourself up to fail.

That day, I set up a spreadsheet and decided what a reasonable – but challenging – monthly goal would be. I had my prospects on one side and my sales on the other. I also purchased a large dry erase board, and wrote top prospects on one side and closed sales on the other. To keep myself on task, I put it right in front of me so I could see it all day, every day.

Next, I signed up for Google's Zoho app that offers a free customer retention management platform to set up my database. That's where I organized my client and prospects lists, so I could call them up at any time. It helped me organize my daily prospecting and provided reminders for following up. Eventually, I learned how much prospecting I had to do to achieve the result I needed to make my revenue goal.

So just in case you're saying to yourself, "Oh, it was easy for her. She's a professional salesperson." Get over yourself. If you're going to own a business, you *will* be a salesperson, whether you have the experience or not! It's never *easy*, regardless of your background.

After getting my database organized, I set up what would end up being the marketing tool that catapulted my business: an email newsletter. (*We'll talk more about this in a later chapter.*)

This was a huge turning point for my business. After three months of religiously practicing my newly structured routine, things started to happen for SocialHeavy. I was starting to create a profitable business.

I recently read somewhere that 70 percent of women-owned businesses never break $50,000 in annual profit. If you don't want to be just another statistic, I strongly suggest setting financial milestones and having a structured plan you work every single day.

CHAPTER TEN

Building Your Pipeline

When you start your own venture, your list of clients and prospective clients is essentially the heart of your business.

If I talk to ten small business owners at random – whether they've been in business for 3 months or 7 years – and ask them about their database, I'll hear crickets from at least 7 of them. A popular response is, "It's in my Outlook." While that's better than nothing, it is *not* the proper tool to build a strategic sales funnel and track customer relationships.

It's crucial when your business is new to start up systems and processes that create and track profitability. It can get more complicated once you have been in business for a while. If something is difficult and time consuming people tend to put it off, but not having a well-organized database is going to cost you sales and inhibit your company's growth.

"Having the proper systems in your business is crucial!"

You'll need to use a CRM, or Customer Retention Management, platform. I recommend using a web-based application, so you'll never worry about your computer crashing and losing your information. I've used Google's free Zoho app for years, and I love it because you can divide your list by prospects and clients, make notes, and properly document the sales cycle. Another thing I love about Zoho is the customization factor. For example, you can break down your customer contacts by industry, and industry-focused selling is *very powerful!* You can also grade your prospects to help identify your best opportunities at a glance and navigate the sales process with ease.

My personal grading system works as follows:

- **Active Prospect** – I've done the proper research on the prospect, and they appear to fit my client profile. More importantly, it's clear the prospect needs my services.

- **Qualified Pipeline** – I've reached out to the prospect, and they've signaled interest. A sign of interest would be agreeing to accept extended information on my company or agreeing to a phone call or a meeting to get acquainted.

- **Hot Pipeline** – I have met or spoken with the contact, and they're genuinely interested in doing business with me. Now, it's just a matter of closing the sale. This is where great follow-up comes into play because most people lose a ton of new opportunities because they don't follow up! Some prospects – even though they've given a nod of genuine interest – don't pull the trigger right away. Stay in close communication with them until you make the sale.

- **Customer** - Hurray! I've taken the contact all the way through the process, and they've just become my customer. However, it doesn't end there! Once you've completed the sale or project with your new customer, you *must* stay in touch! The best customers are always going to be the ones you already have. You should be able to pull up all of your customers with ease and check to see the last time you touched base with them. Come up with a new product or idea? Great! Call everyone that you've already done business with. You'll have your best opportunities for sales there.

- **Cold Prospect** – I was unable to make a connection with the prospect due to no response. Also, this category is for hot leads that go cold, meaning I couldn't turn them into customers. Hey it happens! (But not often, thank goodness!) Sometimes people get cold feet and revert back to the beginning of the process. I usually follow up again with them in 30 days, depending on the situation.

The purpose of a well-built database is to have a tool that provides a map leading to sales success! The objective is to move the contact all the way through the process until they reach the pipeline. Then, it's a matter of turning them into a client.

Your pipeline, by the way, is a list of contacts with the potential to become clients in the near future, and you should know it backwards and forwards at ALL times.

I know you'd rather have a root canal, but if you'd spend just one week getting your database together and organized properly, I guarantee your return on investment will be staggering!

CHAPTER ELEVEN

Pick a Lane

One of the biggest mistakes I made when I started SocialHeavy was thinking I'd succeed as long as I had a product to sell – to everyone. If I could sell to everyone, I couldn't possibly fail, right?

Wrong!

Starting a business is a very tough undertaking, especially if you're funding it yourself and living on a hope and a prayer the way I was. You are *not* going to have the luxury of making crap decisions, so listen up!

Your days are going to consist of:

- Developing and marketing your business.
- The day-to-day stuff like bookkeeping and planning.
- Taking care of the customers and the work you already have.
- Then guess what? You still have to go out and get new business!

In the beginning you'll have a much higher success rate if you choose one thing you do very well and become the best at it you can possibly be. You want to be thought of as the go-to person for whatever that is. Then, to increase your chances of success even further, target one or two specific industries. Now, here's the tricky part: Don't think about what *you* need to sell. Think about what *they* need to buy!
If you choose the restaurant industry, for example, become an expert. What are the problems facing restaurant owners? What keeps them

up at night? What do they need to run their business better? How does your business fit into the picture?

Then, you'll need to calculate how much your company's worth to your chosen industry. This "value proposition", or your personal promise of the quality and delivery of a top-notch product or service, will not only play an integral role in building a brand, but will also become a large part of your marketing strategy.

> *"Being an expert at something very specific is a huge advantage."*

Another strategy is to use competition to your advantage. If you find yourself competing against another company for business, but you serve that particular industry explicitly, and the other guy doesn't, you could potentially have an edge over them.

One of the greatest values in picking a lane is the stress it alleviates when it comes down to business development, or the actual art of selling. When I set SocialHeavy up to be a virtual company, I thought one of the coolest things about it was the lack of conventional boundaries. I had this endless sea of prospects just ripe for the plucking! I could sell to anyone in the world!

Guess what?

I lost count of the hours I spent just sitting at my desk, staring at my computer wondering what the hell I was going to do next. Who was I going to call? There were too many choices. I didn't know where to start.

So I didn't. I avoided doing sales because it was just too hard, and my business suffered.

It became very obvious to me that the world was just too big of a place for me to take on. I needed boundaries! I had to figure out very quickly how to focus on a much smaller target; otherwise I was going to fail – again.

When I made the decision to scale back my offerings and do industry-targeted marketing, it made the day-to-day much easier. Having a clear focus of who I was selling to and what I was going to sell them made me much more productive. And what happens when you're productive? Yep. Your chances of success rise significantly!

CHAPTER TWELVE

Marketing – Finding Your Perfect Equation

Marketing isn't something you can just do for a day or so and expect rewards. If you don't put forth the effort and don't get the results you want, don't blame the process. *You* didn't work the process.

In other words, you can't treat marketing like a booty call! If you're not selling your product, you don't have a business.

So what is marketing exactly? Marketing can have different meanings, depending on whom you ask. Webster's defines it as the action or business of selling and promoting products or services.

On average, business owners spend only about 15 percent of their time doing marketing and the remaining 85 percent caught up in tasks that don't create revenue. If you are in growth mode and need more business that scenario needs to be flipped. You should be spending the majority of your time – everyday – doing activities that are directly related to growing your business' revenue.

With social media and digital marketing on the scene we have many methods to get the word out about our businesses fast. However, it's important that you don't rely on those tools alone, traditional marketing methods such as networking and just plain picking up the phone need to be used in the mix as well. The key is figuring out the right blend of methods that work best for *your* business, or *your* "Perfect Equation".

What is the Perfect Equation?
The Perfect Equation is the combination of the marketing tools you use together to create the desired profitability in your business. Building your Perfect Equation means you know exactly what your marketing strategy needs to be to grow your business and push it forward.

The marketing tools you use to find your equation will be influenced by your business model. This is where knowing your target market comes into play. Who are you selling to? How can you reach them in large numbers? What are their needs? What problems can you solve for them?

Not every marketing method is right for every business, so you'll need to consider a variety of available tools such as email and video marketing, blog publishing, click-through Internet ads and networking – including both traditional marketing methods and embracing social media.

How do you find your Perfect Equation? It takes commitment, experimentation, and lots of trial and error. Most entrepreneurs get stumped because they want the rewards great marketing brings, but they have difficulty committing to the time it takes to create it.

I can't tell you how often people tell me social media, for example, doesn't work for their business. It only takes a few questions to discover it didn't work for them because they didn't understand how to use it and they didn't have a strategy.

You can't just post on Facebook and Twitter without a consistent marketing strategy and expect to get results. That's like me working out in the morning and then eating a cheesecake and drinking a bottle of wine every night and then blaming my personal trainer because I'm fat. It's not his fault that I'm fat! It's my fault because I gave my diet a half-assed effort.

Have a Plan in Place – and Work It!

When it comes to marketing, you have to operate within a structured framework, stay within that structure and consistently follow through.

Social media, for example, is about communicating and sharing information that's interesting, solves problems and educates others. The content you share shouldn't be self-serving. The value of social media is the sharing aspect. If people like your content they're likely to share it with their followers, and if their followers like it, they'll share it, too. This is what's known as "viral marketing," the phenomenon that makes social media the most incredible marketing opportunity of our lifetime.

Ask yourself this question: "What do I want to happen by using social media?"

The idea is structuring a plan that makes that action happen. In *my personal* Perfect Equation, one way I use social media is to generate referral traffic, or the traffic arriving at your site from another source. We all need to drive traffic to our websites to be seen, create leads, and make sales. Social media is brilliant for driving website traffic, and with the right strategy you can actually increase your traffic significantly overnight. It's that fast!

One thing to consider in your marketing strategy is that the overabundance and traveling speed of information has given people the attention spans of gnats. Once they get to your website they need to know exactly what you want them to do. It's critical that you make sure it's very clear. If you say, "I want them to buy," for example, make sure the path to purchasing is very obvious. Try using big, bold letters in multiple locations that say, "Click Here to Purchase."

Another thing to consider is while we want information quickly, we're still pretty slow when it comes to actually purchasing anything, especially if it's a higher-ticket item.

You may not sell anything to your visitor right away, however there is another form of currency that is just as valuable as making the sale that you should be focusing on. You will want to collect their email address for your list.

Your website should be used for the following purposes:

- To create awareness and educate about the value of what you sell.
- To brand your business in a way that stands out from your competition.
- To connect people with you or your business on a personal level.
- To sell your product or service.
- To capture email addresses, so you can grow your marketing list.

Your List
Your list is your power. It is the very core of profitability AND the source of your control in your business. Growing your list is the core of your Perfect Equation. If you don't have a good list of people to market to on a regular basis, there's a huge hole in your plan.

How will you get those email addresses? A very important tool in your marketing strategy is going to be "email capture". One idea is to place valuable information on your website that is free to the visitor. This information should be of interest to your target market and is a solution to an obstacle in their business or serves as a how-to of sorts. This information is commonly referred to as a "white paper," or an authoritative report or guide that helps to solve a problem. They can receive the information by downloading it from your website. Once they do, you've captured their email address.

Next, you should have a very visible place where your visitors can sign up for newsletters. Another way to capture email addresses is to allow your visitors to subscribe to your blog. Whenever you write a new blog post it is emailed to them.

As you can see, there are multiple ways to capture email addresses from your website and ideally you should use them all. Multiple sign-ups are useful because visitor interest will vary. Some may be interested in your download, while others may just want to receive the newsletter.

There are other ways to get email addresses such as networking, holding webinars, and attending events. You should constantly be focused on growing the list.

> *"Your list is the source of profitability in your business."*

Every tool you use in your Perfect Equation has one purpose and that is to provide leads to fill your pipeline and grow your list. The bigger your list is, the bigger your pipeline. The bigger your pipeline is, the more opportunities for sales. If you expand your sales, you grow your business!

As a result it is a very good idea to have a goal every month on how many email addresses you intend on increasing your list by.

Growing your list is like increasing your paycheck!

Email marketing is an amazing opportunity to do just that, and I'm shocked that so few businesses use it. In 2011, my email newsletter catapulted my business! Once you send out a newsletter you can go back later and see tangible evidence of interest in your business by viewing the analytic reports. You can see who opened it, how many times, and if they clicked through to connect with your further, like your website for example.

I wrote *Yanking Bootstraps* as a guide to assist entrepreneurs in growing their businesses and preventing unnecessary mistakes. When I came up with the outline, I took pieces of the content and published it in my email newsletter, which is a subscriber base made up of mainly entrepreneurs. If it had a high open rate, I could tell the topic was interesting and helpful to my audience. If numerous readers opened it multiple times, this told me they were relating to it, and the topic was a hit. It's one thing to think you have content that's good enough for a book, but it's a whole other thing if your target audience thinks it's good. Talk about market research!

So what if you don't currently have a strategy in place to build your list?

Let me give you a bullet-by-bullet list of things you should do ASAP to get started.

- Gather all your emails into one place and put them into a spreadsheet that you will upload to a newsletter platform.
- Set up your newsletter.
- Write a report or white paper that distinguishes itself as valuable information to your niche market for download from your website.
- Set up sign-ups on your website for your newsletter, your blog posts or to download your information or white papers.
- Set a monthly goal for growing the email list.

If you take anything at all away from this book, let it be this: *Your list is the source of profitability in your business*. Consistently build it, and watch your business grow!

CHAPTER THIRTEEN

Stay the Course

We've all heard the phrase, "Stay the course" – usually in reference to military action – but the saying has slowly made its way into everyday lingo whenever we talk about working through obstacles or criticism.

The expression becomes especially appropriate when we talk about self-employment because it certainly feels like a war zone at times.

It helps to avoid the curse of the Three D's: defeat, distraction and discouragement. At best, they'll suck your energy, and have you running around in unproductive circles. At worst, they'll cause your failure.

> *"Being an entrepreneur is certainly not for the weak-hearted."*

Like any business owner, I occasionally have a week that's a major suck-fest! A project I spent lots of time on and *thought* was a good idea turns out to be a dud, so I kick myself over lost time. I've also had times when I couldn't close sales that I thought were a sure thing. In times of sheer exhaustion, I've looked at myself in the mirror and said, "You are stupid for thinking you can make this business work, and you need to get a real job!"

You know what I learned? It's only a temporary setback. The next week, I'd come up with an even better idea for a new product; I'd close sales; and once again, faith in myself would be restored.

Having gone through this process more than a few times, I learned that if I just put my head down, plow through and stick to my game plan no matter what, everything turns out fine.

It helps that I've adopted the mindset and attitude of a warrior.

Think of yourself as a Roman gladiator, standing in the middle of the Colosseum preparing to fight a wild beast. There's only one problem: You don't have a sword or a shield. Think of your marketing plan as your shield and sword. Without it you're unprepared for battle and your demise is very likely.

Even armed with the most brilliant marketing plan imaginable, however, you'll still most likely face one of the Three D's on occasion. It just comes with the territory.

Here are some ways to combat them:

1. **Defeat**. You must go into entrepreneurship being mentally prepared for hardship and obstacles. There are going to be times you'll fail. This is when a strong mindset comes into play. You *must* have faith in yourself and a strong passion for your business. You *must* believe with all your heart in what you're doing and why you're doing it. Failure doesn't have to be negative. It can just as easily become an opportunity to learn to be better and stronger. Without failure, we never learn to cope with adversity. Learning to thrive despite adversity is an imperative skill for today's entrepreneur. Without it you cannot succeed.

2. **Distraction**. To combat distraction you must create boundaries, especially with your family and friends. You need to explain to your family, for example, that just because you're home, doesn't mean you aren't working. Your children should be taught to be respectful of your work. Your friends

need to understand that you're busy and don't have time to "do" lunch. If your friends call during your working hours, don't answer. Call them back later. Something that really helps me is making a list for the next day every night before I go to bed. The list is organized by high-payoff actions first, so if some of the little things don't get done because of an interruption, it's not life or death. Also, make sure you make some time each day for yourself to mediate, exercise or do something you enjoy. This will give you the mental boost needed to stay productive.

3. **Discouragement.** This is my least favorite of the Three D's. In my personal opinion, it is the hardest from which to rebound. I combat this with the company I keep, surrounding myself with people who are positive, successful and supportive when I'm feeling unmotivated. Also, ask yourself, how bad is it *really*? Try to add some positivity to the situation. Are you making things worse than they really are? What is the worst that could happen?

Being an entrepreneur is certainly not for the weak-hearted. If you enter the arena armed with a warrior's attitude, though, you just may find yourself in the winner's circle!

Expert Insight: Neen James
Productivity expert, professional speaker, mentor, author

"As entrepreneurs we need to learn to Fold Time™ - achieve twice as much in half the time! Being fully accountable for how we invest time, engaging in activities that require our undivided attention and leveraging everything we do by managing our energy."

"My secret is to apply the 15-minute rule. It is easy to get distracted, so set yourself (and a timer) to work on a project for just 15 minutes – you will be astounded at what you can achieve in 15 dedicated (not multi-tasked) minutes."

"Another social media management distraction strategy is to only check social media on your mobile devices – this allows you to stay focused on what you are working on."

"You don't have time to do everything. You only have time to do what matters!"

CHAPTER FOURTEEN

Take Action!

Is there someone you know who seems much more successful than you? Ever wonder, "Why doesn't it happen for me?" or "Why is it so easy for them, yet so hard for me?"

Chances are, the only thing standing in your way is *you*.

First of all, it isn't easy for them either, no matter how it seems from the outside looking in. I can personally assure you of that. So why do you think they have a step up on you?

Perhaps they're smarter? Maybe.

Maybe they have better connections? Possibly.

Is it simply because they're better looking? It's not entirely out of the question, considering some studies *have* shown that very attractive people tend to be the most successful. I'm just sayin'....

I've been in the business world a very long time. I've met many different people from various walks of life, businesses and mindsets. I'm not saying it's true in *all* cases, but the usual reason one person is more successful than another has nothing to do with looks, connections or even intelligence.

One word separates the few from most: Action.

Successful people take action!

They understand the power of *now*, and embrace a mindset that pushes them past mediocrity toward a higher level of success.

Have you ever caught yourself saying, "Once I _____ , then I'll _____."

Does the first blank *ever* get done?

Most of the people I talk to always have an excuse or something they'd rather do before taking that next step to grow their business. Problem is, the obstacle they've *purposely* placed in the way never gets done.

There are certain tasks we want to get done that have no *real* effect on our business. For example, getting a cooler business card designed. That's nice, and you should do that, but it's not going to stunt business growth if you put it off.

"One word separates few from most: Action."

The worst self-inflicted diversion, however, is busy work.

Busy work is nothing but a mechanism to keep you on the hamster wheel. Wasting time on busy work gives you a false sense of accomplishment, and it's easy to get caught up in it. I'm reminded of this quote by Benjamin Franklin, *"Never confuse motion with action."*

What about doing a better job of marketing yourself? What about working harder at business development or sending out that newsletter you've never gotten around to finishing? Perhaps you'd feel more accomplished creating a stronger, more visible brand or a better website that truly showcases your business?

All these things create growth in your business and do, indeed, have a real effect. So here's my question: Did giving whatever you wrote in that first blank priority over the second directly grow your business? It should!

Here are 5 ways to take action in your business:

1. **Put a dollar sign on your time.** It's imperative you realize your time costs money. How are you spending it? Are you creating revenue, or are you distracting yourself with administrative tasks?

2. **Have a plan.** Set a monthly revenue goal, and schedule activity every day toward reaching it.

3. **Don't wait.** Conditions will never be perfect. Now is always the best time. Waiting is just an excuse. Successful people don't sit around all day making excuses; they move forward.

4. **Get a coach.** A coach will help you figure out your action plan and, more importantly, will hold you accountable, so you follow through.

5. **Avoid over-planning.** One thing I've learned these past few years is that entrepreneurs love to plan! They get out their fancy notebooks and map out their marketing strategy. There's nothing wrong with that, mind you. The problem is they plan it to death, and planning doesn't grow your business. Implementing a good plan grows your business. Be an implementer not a planner!

6. **Don't be so intimidated by the success of others.** You *can* have what they have if you *really* want it.

CHAPTER FIFTEEN

Your Pricing Strategy

Just about anyone who starts a business struggles with pricing. Actually, it may always be a struggle in today's economy. Everything has become more about price than quality, and some people make the huge mistake of basing their buying decisions on price alone.

In the beginning it's imperative to build a client base that will provide you with referrals. Why? When you have great feedback, people will trust you and want to do business with you.

Referrals are the quickest way to build a business today due largely to the power of social media. Make a client really happy, and they'll tell everyone who follows them about their experience with your business.

The result is *social proof,* or informational social influence, which can make a significant impact on the success and growth of your business. Social proof is a physiological phenomenon where people assume that because others they admire and trust are listening to or doing business with someone, then they should as well. In turn, you're judged by the number of people following you on Facebook and Twitter, and the process is only going to become more prevalent in the future.

That's why it's extremely important to do extensive research before pricing your products and services. You'll need to decide where you want to be in the marketplace and what types of clients you want to attract. Then, design a strategy that matches that decision, and stand firm. Compromising your pricing can confuse buyers and damages both your brand and reputation.

Your pricing considerations are:

- **Low-tier**. Here, your intention is to do business with anyone and everyone, creating a high-volume business dependent on the frequency of low-profit sales. Unfortunately in today's economy, this pricing strategy has become the most common. The quality of service and expertise has started to decline. People have learned to pay less while expecting more; the buyer in most cases ends up being very disappointed with the purchase. Some buyers only see the price tag and think they are saving money; they fail to analyze the consequences of the cheapest choice.

- **Mid-tier**. In this pricing strategy you are middle-of-the-road: not the cheapest guy and not the most expensive. This strategy favors startups as it gives you the most flexibility for future growth. Not being the cheapest helps you build a little more of a brand, but you're not pricing yourself out of your market either.

- **High-end**. This strategy focuses exclusively on the high-end buyer. In order to sell in this category you'll need to be extremely service-oriented (*we're talking red carpet*) and having social proof will essential. High-end is a quality-over-quantity strategy because there are fewer customers. However, they will pay more. If you choose this route out of the gate just know that selling to this market will be extremely difficult without customer testimonials and a large following. You will also need to resist the urge to compromise in times of desperation. It can damage your reputation irreparably.

Above all, don't forget your *sales cycle*. In Chapter 10 we talked about the various levels of the pipeline, or the process of moving a qualified lead from prospect to customer. The sales cycle is the length of time it takes to do that. If your product or service is a large investment for the buyer, you're going to have a longer sales cycle. Not only will you have to work harder to make a sale, but it increases the likelihood of creating longer gaps between sales. The lack of consistent cash flow has caused more than its share of business failures.

If your business model allows, provide a cost option for every tier. Then, it's not a matter of the client saying yes or no, but merely choosing an option. This strategy works because it maintains both short- and long-sales cycles, keeping revenue flow consistent.

Of course, if people don't understand or value what you do or sell, they won't purchase it at *any* price. That's why its important to use tools such as blogging and social media. You need to create content that sets you apart from competitors and positions you as a leader in your field. The content you create should contain solutions to your ideal clients' problems. This is a process commonly referred to as *pull marketing*. Rather than pushing your business on people, this process pulls them in, creating value and loyalty that becomes the foundation for lasting business relationships.

"Pull marketing is the process of pulling your ideal client toward you, as opposed to pushing your message on them."

On the downside, pull marketing tends to take an investment of time on the front end. More entrepreneurs tend to be attracted to push marketing because they feel hitting the pavement asking people to buy is more proactive. They feel that because they're working harder, the payment will be higher. They are wrong.

Pull marketing may not produce an immediate return, but this investment will make business easier to get over time. It also generates awareness; creating the leverage you need to charge more for your product in the future.

CHAPTER SIXTEEN

The Crazies – Turning Down Bad Business

There is another consideration when choosing a pricing strategy for your business. The pricing structure you pick is going to attract a certain buyer, and you need to decide: Is that the buyer you want?

In the beginning, you want business. You need revenue, and you don't care who's supplying it. I know. I've been there, and let me tell you: The crazies are more trouble than they're worth!

We all get a crazie from time to time, that customer who makes unreasonable demands, needs an extraordinary amount of hand-holding, doesn't pay on time, costs us more time than they paid for, and actually wreaks havoc on our well-being by causing us emotional grief.

Fortunately, for me they've been rare, allowing for a nice recovery in between occurrences. In preparing to write this chapter, though, I decided to make a list of my crazies. Over the past three years I've encountered five. This number would be much higher if I hadn't learned how to spot and dodge them. The common denominator? They all came in at a very low price point.

Interesting? Yes. Coincidence? No.

Some – but not all – customers who come in at a cheap price tend to have a very low threshold for assigning value to anything. And because they don't believe in paying for a high level of service, they aren't accustomed to receiving a higher level of communication and professionalism. As a result of their lack of experience doing business at a higher level, you get treated like crap.

A book I absolutely love that has a permanent spot on my nightstand is called *The Pumpkin Plan* by Mike Michalowicz. In his seven-step process of growing a successful business, step three is firing all of your rotten clients. I couldn't agree more! He talks about how you should do business with people you want to work with, who give you the most business, have reasonable expectations and communicate well.

> *"You'll need to consider your reputation when dealing with a crazie."*

As you are designing the framework that's going to grow your business and take it to the next level, a consideration needs to be the types of clients you're attracting. If these clients are stunting your growth and holding you back, you *must* send them packing!

A good way to avoid the crazies is to spot them in the beginning. Anytime you have a business that involves a service extending past an immediate purchase and "Thank you, come again," you should have a qualification process. Before you're locked into spending an extended amount of time with someone, you need to make sure they're a good fit for your business – not a money-drain and not going to make you want to kill little kittens.

How to spot a crazie:

- If they're focused on price the entire conversation and don't ask questions that are important to see if you're actually even a fit for their business, this is a red flag. Run.

- If they're rude or condescending during the first chat, chances are they will be on the next. Send them packing!

- If they're extremely indecisive and have absolutely no idea what product or service they need – be warned. You have yourself a hand-holder. This could turn out to be a good client; however, if you proceed, do *not* sell to this person at a low price point. They're going to require a lot of your time.

- If they mention several of your peers they tried to work with but fired because they weren't good enough, save yourself! The client who can't be pleased is the worst offender of them all.

- If they have unrealistic expectations, forget about it, especially if they say the words "*I want*" 10 times within one paragraph.

- If they have a huge sense of urgency and want everything yesterday, this person is about to make your life a living hell. You may as well go back to corporate America because they're going to add a ton of stress, insisting on unrealistic deadlines.

- If when pressed for a payment they say, "Oh, it was mailed back to me. I accidently got your zip code wrong", you've got bigger problems. You don't need a crystal ball to prove missing checks will be a regular part of your future.

I could go on and on! Simply put, screen your prospective clients well, and try not to think with your wallet. Instead, decide if this person is a good fit for you long term. What you don't want is a client that is going to make you a candidate for alcohol abuse counseling.

Lastly, but maybe most importantly, you'll need to consider your reputation when dealing with a crazie. If you're not careful and don't do everything just right, they could say bad things about you that could damage your business.

Let's not forget, especially in today's world with social media, everyone is a publisher and has an audience. You may know this person is missing some tools in the shed, but does everyone else?

CHAPTER SEVENTEEN

Ignorance is **NOT** Bliss

To be a successful entrepreneur today, one essential trait matters most: the ability to evolve.

The business world is driven by fast-changing technology, and as an entrepreneur, *you* are the force driving your business. As a result, you have a responsibility to learn to use the tools designed specifically to impact your business' growth and future success.

I can't tell you how many business owners I talk to who completely reject technology. It's no surprise that they struggle in their business because they're missing selling opportunities found only by knowing how to leverage the power of the Internet.

Additionally, there are many technology-driven devices and applications that can save you tons of time and money by making your business more efficient. I'm not suggesting you become a guru or a techie. What I am suggesting is that if you're going to succeed in today's business environment, you *must* be willing to adapt to change.

For example, if you find that your website isn't getting the proper traffic, you might need to hire a search engine optimization expert. For the unfamiliar, search engine optimization is the process of improving the visibility, ranking, traffic and search results from web search engines like Google.

And at some point, you'll have to purchase technology-driven services and products for your business. If you're on your own and don't have an IT department at your disposal, it's a good idea to be educated at least enough that you understand what you're purchasing. Don't get screwed over by someone trying to sell you something you don't need.

It's always a good idea to start with online research and obtain a basic understanding of the products you're buying. If you're even minimally educated to the point that you were able to have an intelligent conversation that lets the salesperson know you're not totally in the dark, you can save yourself some money and avoid getting ripped off! But be very careful. The Internet is crawling with marketers who prey on the ignorance of uneducated buyers.

The ability to understand the advantages of social media and capitalize on this incredible marketing opportunity, however, is huge for your business. If you're visibly out of the game and your competitors aren't, guess who comes out ahead? More importantly, ignorance of the Internet alienates digital-savvy buyers, and can you really afford that?

"You can't close your eyes, put your fingers in your ears and say LA LA LA LA."

With all the free online resources at your disposal, you literally have no excuse not to learn. Just simply type a topic of interest into the Google search and you will have tons of information returned. Another great resource for learning is YouTube. You can find a YouTube video tutorial for just about anything imaginable!

Here are a few tips for becoming more tech savvy:

- Change your mindset! If you have a mental wall up against learning something, you'll never learn it, no matter how hard you try.

- Dedicate at least one hour a week to reading and learning. Research a specific topic you'd like to become more educated about.

- Find people on the Internet and follow their blogs. There are tons of experts that you can follow and learn from.

- Enroll in an online course if you feel you need something beyond self-structured learning.

- Join a discussion group on LinkedIn.

Face it. The world around you is changing. You can't close your eyes, put your fingers in your ears and say LA LA LA LA. It won't help.

You have to tear down your mental walls, get past your fears, change your mindset and adapt.

Expert Insight: Gina Schreck
Social marketing expert, speaker, author

"The future is HERE! It's just not evenly distributed."

"As a business owner, I want to make sure I am always in the front or as close to the front as possible when it comes to knowing how to help my customers. If they are coming to me with ideas for building their business with technology tools that I have never even heard of, I move to the back of the line."

"There is no excuse anymore for not taking the time to learn – as Tammy said, we have all the information we could possibly need, at our fingertips. Stay on top of your industry and as close to the front of the pack as possible. Read, watch or listen to everything you can get your hands on that will make you a valuable resource to your clients and potential clients."

"If you are still clinging to the excuse that you just don't have the time, then you don't want it bad enough. I get frustrated when I hear people say, "I would do anything to be as successful as so-and-so." I say, go ask that person what they do that has given them that level of success, and then DO IT! I guarantee they are not laying out tanning themselves and watching Judge Judy."

"Put in the time sharpening your skills to be the very best in your industry instead of watching television, instead of reading junk magazines, read about what is going on in your field. Watch or listen to one podcast per week, and you will rise to the top and be seen as a thought leader in your industry. You can sleep when you're dead!"

CHAPTER EIGHTEEN

Branding: The Size of a Mouse with the Roar of a Lion

Technology has leveled the playing field. The digital world makes size hard to distinguish at face value because it gives small and large businesses, alike, an equal online presence.

After a year into SocialHeavy, I was doing quite well and my work was widely recognized. I attribute that to three things: clients who loved my work and shared me with their friends, strategic marketing, and putting myself out there in a big way.

In the beginning when no one knew me from Adam's house cat, I branded myself as if I were a big player. Was I pretending? Of course not! I *was* a big player but nobody knew it yet.

I made sure I stood out and that no matter where you saw me on the Internet, you experienced the same vision of my business. I decided what my desired outcome was, and I emulated it as reality. I manifested a brand, and with hard work to back it up, it came to pass.

Sadly, it really wasn't that challenging to stand out.

Only the big dogs tend to create a bold Internet presence. I will never understand that. Many small business owners think that great branding is reserved for the Starbucks and Targets of the world.

It's not. Decide what you want. Decide how you want people to see you, and manifest that in an obvious and courageous way. If you don't first see it in yourself, how do you expect others to?

Standing out in a digital world
Social media has created a major shift in the way we communicate and market ourselves. Now, everyone has a voice and the opportunity to be a publisher. Bad news? The world is quite noisy now. You have to do something to stand out; otherwise, it's just too easy to look like everyone else and not be heard.

If you ignore branding yourself, you're just shouting out against the noise. Imagine pouring water into a bucket with a hole in the bottom. Without the proper branding strategy that's what your marketing efforts are going to accomplish.

"Perception is, indeed, reality!"

Another thing to consider is how high you reach when you do decide to brand yourself. A while back a client of mine with a really small practice mentioned that no one she felt equivalent to was branding themselves the way I was coaching her to. She felt uncomfortable putting herself out there this way. My response to her was you never emulate who you think you fit in with; you emulate who you want to be, and you walk that path until it becomes your reality.

It's not just tangible things like logos and websites that create a brand. It's you. It's how you present yourself to your client, your level of professionalism, and a contagious passion for your business. When your unique way of presenting information to your followers and clients sets you apart, that's your brand.

Give yourself an edge
A lot of people don't want to put themselves out there because they fear others will steal their work. There are an endless amount of lazy shirttail-riders out there. The Internet is there for everyone to see, so it's easy for them to do.

I have quite a few "stalkers" myself! But you know what? They can twist my words into their own, but they can't *be* me. Great branding sets you apart and makes you very hard, if not impossible, to copy.

A great branding strategy can give you an edge over your competitor. Sometimes even if they've been in business longer and are bigger, you can create a crushing presence. How does a lightweight tool like a jack lift something as heavy as a car? It's called leverage. You can use that same concept to beat out your competitor using branding as your jack.

Take a look at the tangible things that represent your business. Do they adequately communicate your passion and expertise? Do they tell people who you are? Does it equal your level of professionalism? Does it match your value to your target market? Always remember: Perception is, indeed, reality!

You may not have a big budget for marketing right now, and that's okay. Start small with things like stationery and business cards, but make sure you do a fantastic job branding those things you *can* afford. Details are very important.

If you look hard enough, you can almost always find someone in your price range. Just make sure they understand branding and are a good fit for you. Take a look at the way they brand their own business. If it looks crappy, and they don't walk their talk, find someone else. If you put in an effort you will find the right person to fit your needs *and* budget. The effort is worth it, remember *this is* your business we are talking about.

CHAPTER NINETEEN

The Real Cost of Doing Business with Your Friends

In starting your new business with practically zero budget for marketing, you may think it's a great idea to solicit the services of a friend to save money because you can't afford a professional. I've found that – in most cases – involving friends in your business just to help them out or save a buck is a *very* bad idea. It almost never works out the way you plan.

This is something a lot of people who bootstrap their businesses do. Actually, I deal with it often, and it usually sounds like this: *"I hired my friend to do my website because I didn't have much money, and I thought they could do it."*

Guess what? They paid their friend and then ended up paying me to fix it. Yep, you do the math. They actually ended up paying more after all.

I had someone contact me about a website a while back, and we talked about the one he already had which was done by his friend. The site was a complete disaster. It didn't look the way he wanted it to, it looked very amateurish in comparison to others in his industry. More importantly, his friend didn't know anything about search engine optimization, so it wasn't Internet friendly. Not to mention, his friend told him it would take him four weeks to build it, but it took eight months!

I asked him why he let his friend do it in the first place, and he said that his buddy needed the work, and he offered him a deal that saved him $1,500 compared with the professional web developer's quote. Then I asked him why did it take so long, and why did he let him get away with it? He said his buddy had to take a second job, and was having a hard time, he didn't want to make things worse for him.

So let's see: He got a cheap website that wasn't built properly, and it took him eight months to bring it online. After the money spent, the frustration involved in waiting, and the time lapse that stalled his business' launch, he didn't even get what he wanted.

The real question he had to ask himself was – when it was all said and done – how much did this website really cost him?

"The vendor relationships you have need to be strictly professional."

When it comes to your business, you really need to take things that represent it and sell it seriously. The vendor relationships you have need to be *strictly professional.* You don't want to be in a situation where you don't have the upper hand. You also need to consider shaving a few bucks off the front end might end up costing you dearly in the end.

Waiting on something to be done costs you money. Anytime you have to redo something because your buddy didn't do it correctly, that costs you more money.

One of the biggest problems with doing business with your friends is just that: They see you as a friend and not a customer. When they don't see you as a customer, different rules apply, and it seems they feel they don't have to commit to the same level of service. They expect you to cut them some slack.

If you insist on hiring your friend to do something for you in your business, consider these points before going forward. If you answer no to any of these questions, chances are it's not a good idea:

- If you don't like what they do, will you tell them? Would you be as honest with them as you would if you hired a stranger?

- If they are, indeed, a professional, are you willing to pay them the same price you would someone else? You should be. Paying them what they actually charge, without a discount, may cost you more up front, but it gives you leverage. You've started the relationship on a professional standing with the ball in your court.

- Are you going to let your friend's needs trump the needs of your business if this arrangement starts to go badly?

Nobody ever wants to hurt a friend's feelings, but your business must come first in *this* relationship. Making costly mistakes in your business right out of the gate is never ideal, and this is one pitfall you should choose to avoid.

CHAPTER TWENTY

The Middle Part

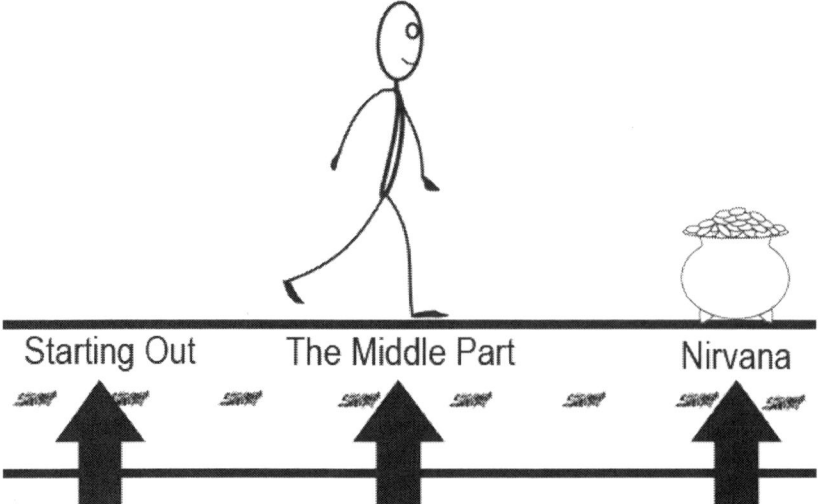

The drawing you see here is a tool I use with my coaching clients to provoke thought. The starting out represents the beginning *or* having to go back to square one, which many businesses face. The middle part is just what it says: You are right there in the middle, and this is when you have to do all the hard work that leads to finding your Nirvana. When you're in the middle, you know what you want to do. You know what it will take to get you there, and you can see it in the distance.

Nirvana is the goal you're working toward. Everyone's Nirvana is different, so it's whatever that means to you.

"If you're going to see real changes, you have to be willing to make some."

The problem is, most entrepreneurs get stuck in the middle and stay there. They managed to get the business to take off okay, and they know what their Nirvana looks like, but they've stopped moving toward it.

Reasons why entrepreneurs stall in the middle:

- **Their own mindset keeps them stuck.** They SAY they want growth, but their actions keep them running in place, and that's where they stay. They don't make the changes necessary to expand, so they're trying to build a bigger business with a small-business mentality. This usually results in unmet goals and spinning wheels.

- **They are too tired by now.** By the time they reach the middle, they're already tired of the climb. You have to be strategic, committed and thorough. What's more, you have to do all this when you *are* tired and feeling a little beat up. When you first start a business, you are low to the ground, so you have no place to go but up. This is the easy part if you can believe that. The hard part comes when you actually get to a place of profitability in your business and *still* have to reach to grow.

- **No plan.** Without a plan for growth, they're just submitting to the business, and many get stuck in the planning stages. These "perpetual planners" enjoy designing a plan; they just never implement it. Planning doesn't grow a business; implementation of a plan does.

- **No accountability.** There is no one holding the paddle and saying, "Okay what's up? Why are we off track?" This happens often with an entrepreneur's business because it's very difficult to police yourself. This is when investing in a business coach is worth it's weight in gold. Everyone needs to be held accountable, and if you are unable to do it for yourself then you need to be smart enough to get the help you need. Without accountability you *will* stand still.

- **Not brave.** They don't invest in their businesses and expand. They usually have one person wearing multiple hats or they have hired people that are not highly qualified just to save a buck. That's okay in the beginning, but at some point you have to take brave steps for growth and invest in smart, intelligent people who can help you take it to the next level. Having people wearing multiple hats creates the "running-around-like-a-chicken-with-its-head-cut-off" situation. In addition hiring an inexperienced person to do a job (*for example your marketing*) just to save money is only hurting yourself and your business. You are purposely delaying the growth of your business. Unfortunately, these business owners rarely experience their Nirvana.

- **Lack of knowledge.** They may know how to run a business, but that's about it. They don't have an understanding of marketing strategy, and they either don't take the time to learn, or they don't invest in someone who does. In today's world of Internet growth and digital technology, it's crucial that entrepreneurs understand how to leverage those resources for the growth of their business.

Over the past four years if I had to pick the most common things that prohibits a business' growth, it's indecision. You will never come across a business owner who doesn't want to grow and make more money. However, there are only a few select entrepreneurs who are willing to step up their game and give it their all. We all want it – but only a few are willing to do something about it.

One thing I know for sure is if you're going to see real changes, you have to be willing to make some. What does your Nirvana look like? Are you taking steps toward it?

CHAPTER TWENTY-ONE

Discovering the Law of Attraction

I went to a very dark place between the failure of my first business and the struggle of getting the second off the ground.

I was exhausted, pissed off and really scared. I was so mad at myself for putting my family's well being in danger, but I was also missing a very important element that had gotten me through a very successful career: I had zero confidence in myself.

The *only* thing that got me through that time was the relentless feeling in my gut that put my feet on the floor every day no matter what. I let it lead me, and even though I felt imprisoned by it at times and had no idea what it wanted me to do, I found the strength to trust it and keep going.

I was at the thrift store one day enjoying one of my favorite pastimes, looking at old books, and I came across a very interesting find: a book called *Living the Law of Attraction: Real Stories of People Manifesting Health, Wealth, and Happiness* by Robin Hoch. I took it home and was immediately sucked in.

Sure, I knew how powerful a mindset can be, but using the law of attraction in my business had never occurred to me. I immediately thought back to a time in the beginning when I consciously parted ways with the negative people in my life. I also reflected on how negative people at different times in my life had made me doubt myself and my abilities, how sometimes even certain types of music could bring me to tears.

So I started thinking, if the negative things can have such a real impact on me, then surely the positive things can work as well. I know it sounds rather simple minded, but this is how I reasoned with my inner skeptic to accept this newfound enlightenment.

Stop self-sabotaging
I started reading everything I could get my hands on about the topic, but some of the stories I came across were a little farfetched for me. I don't believe I can bring something into my life by simply willing it to be so. That is ridiculous.

You change your mindset, and your actions create the outcome you want. It's not like you can wave a wand while sitting on your ass and expect everything to be what you always dreamed.

In doing this research, however, I did discover my thoughts had been toxic. I realized I *was* sabotaging myself, and that had to change – yesterday.

> *"Find it inside yourself to get past the fear, self-doubt, and anything else paralyzing you."*

It was around the first of November 2011 when I decided to test the law of attraction. Instead of designing a vision board with pictures of luxury cars, vacation destinations and expensive shoes, I set a financial goal. I wanted my business to make $10,000 in 30 days.

I also decided to wait until November 6 because 30 days from then would be my birthday. If I succeeded, it would be a great thing to celebrate.

This was a very scary goal given I was only seven months into my new business, and it was rare for me to make more than $3,000 in one month. I had to prove to myself once and for all that I was capable of raising a successful business, and the goal had to be something I had to stretch to reach. If I failed, I decided that perhaps I should consider returning to the cubicle world.

I pulled out a notebook and wrote down the goal and date. I would write down every sale I make and subtract it from the goal.

The power within

I did what the book said. I started every morning by writing down all the things I was thankful for and found a daily affirmation I could tolerate. Each morning, after I'd made my list I listened to it tell me I was successful, strong, capable and worthy. Admittedly, the first several times I listened to it, I was in tears. I still can't decide why those things were so painful for me to hear, but as time went on, it got easier. I finally started believing my success was possible, and more importantly that I deserved it.

On the first day I found it inside myself to walk the path of my goal as if it were already reality. I tried very hard to conduct my day without fear.

I won't lie. Some days I struggled. Negative thoughts don't leave without a good fight. However, I did the things I knew brought in sales anyway, despite the knot in my stomach. I just kept saying to myself, *"forward Tammy"*, *"move forward anyway"*.

I stayed focused on the goal and kept negative thoughts at bay with my affirmations. When the 30 days ended I'd made $8,700 which I counted as a victory still even though I was a bit short of my goal. Not only was that the most I'd ever made in my own business; I'd proven to myself this really was possible. Now that's a birthday present!

I now knew that I possessed the power within myself to make this business happen. I accepted full responsibility for sabotaging myself in the past. It wasn't that my business hadn't been profitable. There had been a huge obstacle in the way: Me.

I encourage you to try this experiment in your own business, but you must be willing to *fully commit* to it. You have to walk the walk, take action that creates profitability in your business and find it inside yourself to get past the fear, self-doubt, and anything else paralyzing you.

You must have it within yourself to push past mediocrity and stop thinking small. Are you ready to accept the fact that you are capable of something much bigger?

CHAPTER TWENTY-TWO

Rotten Milk: The Case for Failure

I spent a lot of time with my grandparents as a kid, and I didn't realize growing up that my Papa was giving me some of the best business advice I'd ever receive. The impact of his words in my life and in my business today is huge.

One of the stories he told me was about rotten milk.

"Pammy, if you leave the milk out on the counter it will go rotten. If you stick it back in the icebox after it goes rotten, it will get cold, but it's still rotten." (My Papa called me Pammy, but that's a story for another day.)

I remember distinctly at the age of 33, when the significance of this hit me for the first time. Hearing my Papa say this in my head helped me decide it was time to leave my current job and move on.

Wow, my Papa was so smart.

If you're going to be a successful business owner you must possess the ability to spot a mistake, learn your lesson from it and not do it again.

I'm an advocate for failing because some of the best business lessons I've learned were from failure. One of my favorite things to say is *fail well*. I'm a true believer that someone who can pick themselves up right after a hard knock without being a whiney bag and go right back into the pit is capable of greatness.

However, I've had a front row seat on more than one occasion for watching an entrepreneur repeat the same bad behavior and actually expect a different outcome.

"We can't repeat the same bad behaviors in our lives and in our businesses and expect a different outcome."

If your goal is a profitable business, you must create the habits and strategies that provide the results you need for the long haul.

Here are a few examples of rotten milk:

1. **Avoidance.** Doing busy work to avoid what really needs to be done actually creates a false sense of accomplishment that prevents us from having growth in our businesses or our personal lives.

2. **Toxic relationships.** Do you have a business partner that continues to disappoint you? Maybe a friend that is always negative? Do you make excuses for these people to keep them around just so you don't have to deal with finding a *real* solution?

3. **Investments based on short-term thinking.** Have you purchased something in your business just because it was the cheapest or even the easiest choice? In the long run how much did it end up costing you? Or do you keep doing or using something because it cost you money when deep down you know it's the wrong solution? Do you realize it's costing you more and more every day?

4. **Bad clients.** Do you do business with people you know are not your ideal client because it's a quick buck? Did you consider the consequences? Sure you got the money on the front end that you needed, but at what cost?

5. **Denial.** Knowing the business is not working and continuing just because you can't face failure or don't know what else to do. Do you even look at how much your business is making from month to month? Are you afraid that if you do, your dream will be taken away?

We cannot repeat the same bad behaviors in our lives and in our businesses and expect a different outcome. And we simply cannot knowingly use solutions that only temporarily mask a problem.

Remember, you can put the rotten milk back in the fridge, and it *will* get cold. But it's *still* rotten.

CHAPTER TWENTY-THREE

Ten of My Biggest Mistakes

I decided that it would be a great final chapter addition to list all the mistakes I made over the past three years. However, as I started to list them, there were way too many! Instead, listed in no particular order, here are my top 10 mistakes as an entrepreneur:

1. **Not understanding the importance of having a niche.** It's a very hard road when you're trying to sell too many products and services to anyone and everyone. When you have a defined niche it's much easier to choose your ideal client and design strategic marketing messages for that target. You can position yourself as an expert, and as a result, you'll find it much easier to attract clients. Marketing too many different products to too many different types of people is just like throwing wet noodles against the wall to see what sticks.

2. **Not understanding marketing, and not having a plan.** I would say that about 80 percent of the entrepreneurs I've worked with over the past few years didn't understand marketing. You must have a purposeful marketing plan that you can continually use to attract clients to your business. Without marketing your business properly you'll never experience growth (*or your Nirvana*). When I started out in my first business I didn't understand the benefits of email marketing, growing a list, blogging or search engine

optimization. I have no doubt that if I'd been armed with this knowledge, my first business would not have failed.

3. **Being self-indulgent in my marketing efforts.** One of the best things I've ever learned in business is something I call self-removal. Every tool you have that markets your business from website to business cards should cater to what your customer needs to know, not what you want to tell them. There's a huge difference. Your products and services need to be what people need to buy, not what you need to sell. You have to decide who your ideal client is, what they need, and market accordingly.

4. **Waiting for the "perfect" time to do something. Perfection paralysis** is waiting for the perfect time to do something in your business, and is a form of sabotage. You're waiting for something that's never going to happen. For example, it's useless to say, "I'll get more serious about my business when the kids go back to school in the fall." Newsflash: When that obstacle is removed, another will slide into its place. The ability to function well in times of adversity – especially given the current state of our economy – is critical. Don't let chaos distract you. Grow some armor, and move forward.

5. **Allowing myself to be cursed by indecision.** In my opinion, indecision is worse than making a bad decision. The only way you can make a bad decision is having gone forward on something and then found out it was a mistake. In this instance, at least you're moving forward and learning a valuable lesson from the mistake. However, not making any decisions at all is another form of self-sabotage. By standing still in your business you are knowingly delaying growth and learning. Don't fear mistakes. They are just as essential as success.

6. **My mindset was toxic.** I had no idea how much of my failure was self-inflicted until I started studying the law of attraction and realized how truly powerful my mindset was. If

you want to fail, you will. If you want to be inadequate, you will be. The same goes with success. You need to decide exactly what you want from your business, and you must live in that mindset. Act as though it's already reality, and over time, you'll literally transform your environment and your business.

7. **Not understanding the importance of building a list.** Your list is truly the number one asset in your business. You should always be growing the list of people to whom you can market your business every day. Create marketing tools such as downloadable content that is valuable to your target market as a means of capturing their email addresses. Remember: We're in the digital age of marketing now. Build the list, build the list, build the damn list!

8. **Shiny Object Syndrome**. Do you start projects and never finish them? Do you find yourself not knowing which way to go? Do you find yourself intimidated by the success of others so much that it makes you stand still? There's so much going on now with the growth of the Internet and digital marketing, not to mention all the "experts" on the scene. This person is doing something interesting, so you follow them, but oh, this person is doing something interesting too, so now what?

   S.O.S. almost killed my business. And what happens when you do this? Not a damn thing. You accomplish nothing. You should always know what your competitors are doing, however, there is a such thing as overkill. Be aware of your competitors, but have your own plan and move forward in it everyday. Remember, what makes you stand out is you. Be authentic, and be yourself. When you stand out and create a brand, it makes you very hard to copy!

   Here's how I combat S.0.S:

   - My strategic marketing plan is based on research and knowing my own business. When you have a plan you have focus, and you aren't as vulnerable to shiny objects.

- Pick a couple of people who offer the knowledge you seek and follow them exclusively.

- Create a solid niche that keeps you from trying to be to many things to too many people, and you'll hear less noise.

9. **Not having a revenue goal.** Not having a revenue goal is like being lost in the dark without a flashlight. Only when I started setting goals in my business did I start to see growth. You need to know how much revenue you need or want to make, and then it's a matter of setting up a marketing plan that will produce that outcome. In addition, it's crucial that you know how much to the penny your business makes month to month. I can't tell you how many times I've asked a new coaching client how much their business made last month, and I hear crickets! The biggest reason why most entrepreneurs don't set goals is fear. They're afraid they won't make it, and then they have to get real with themselves. The only way to grow a successful business and escape mediocrity is by setting a financial goal and striving to make it.

10. **Bad Clients.** When you're starting out, I know you just want to get business anywhere you can, but it's important you learn to say no. (Think back to Chapter 16, The Crazies) It's also important not to attract clients who are only interested in a low price point. They suck your energy, take away your motivation, and poison your mindset. What's worse, they end up costing you way more than you made. Not to mention, if they're a loose cannon, and you don't do exactly what they want, they can damage your reputation (Remember in the world of social media everyone is a publisher). Trust me: A quick buck is just not worth it.

Expert Insight: Tiffany Denson
Entrepreneur

"I think one mistake I made for so many years was telling others my dreams and listening to all their reasons it would never work instead of my listening to my gut. I am not saying sound advice isn't a wonderful thing, but never let others kill your dream. In so many situations, it is not about the idea but the guts behind it. My dad always told me, 'You must be willing to climb out on the limb to reach the apple.' The willingness to fail is often the key to lasting success!"

Guest Authors

Barbara Corcoran
www.barbaracorcoran.com

Barbara Corcoran's credentials include straight D's in high school and college and twenty jobs by the time she turned twenty-three.

It was her next job that would make her one of the most successful entrepreneurs in the country when she took a $1000 loan to start The Corcoran Group. She parlayed that loan into a five-billion-dollar real estate business, which she sold in 2001 for $66 million. Barbara is also an investor/shark on ABC's reality hit *Shark Tank*, now in its third season. Barbara bought 11 new businesses on the show, which she's now shepherding to success.

Dr. Shannon Reece
www.TheTOPInstitute.com

Sport psychologist, peak performance expert, and former competitive athlete, Dr. Shannon Reece teaches women entrepreneurs and competitive athletes how to leverage their unique assets, and minimize their weaknesses to achieve peak performance.

Her websites, educational products and speaking engagements are built around the fundamentals for success which include, putting yourself at the top of your list of highest priorities without guilt, transforming your fear from a liability into an asset, and understanding that being competitive is not about conforming to the status quo. In 2011, Dr. Reece was voted one of *Forbe's* 25 Most Influential Women Tweeting about Entrepreneurship.

Eliz Greene
www.embraceyourheart.com

Eliz was seven-months pregnant with twins when she suffered a massive heart attack. Her life changed — not only did she survive a ten-minute cardiac arrest, the cesarean delivery of her daughters and open-heart surgery, all on the same day — she gained new perspective and passion for life.

Eliz is a National Spokesperson for the American Heart Association, a professional speaker, and an author.

Natalie MacNeil

www.shetakesontheworld.com

Natalie is an EMMY Award-winning media entrepreneur, influential blogger, and thought leader in the sphere of entrepreneurship and personal branding for women.

She is best known as the Founder and Editor-in-Chief of She Takes On The World, one of the top blogs in the world for entrepreneurial women. She Takes On The World appeared on the *Forbes* list, "Top 10 Entrepreneurial Sites for Women" and the *ForbesWoman* list, "Top 100 Websites for Women." "Natalie is also the author of *She Takes on the World: A Guide to Being Your Own Boss, Working Happy, and Living on Purpose.*"

Neen James

www.neenjames.com

Neen James CSP is a productivity thought leader (and Aussie) who delivers engaging keynotes that have educated, and entertained audiences with real-world strategies that apply at work and life.

She also provides mentoring to women and when she isn't traveling the world on her Harley; she is collecting fabulous shoes!

Nik Lemmens

www.careerjourney.co.uk

Nik began his career working for one of the most recognized companies in the world, Apple Computer. There he learned two important lessons; provide excellent service and have fun while you do it.

After progressing into management Nik acquired his MBA and moved into management consulting advising business owners and directors of large corporations on how to improve their businesses. In addition, Nik works as a career coach to clients all over the globe and has developed a very unique approach in helping his clients climb the ladder to their desired career.

Gina Schreck
www.synapse3di.com

Gina Schreck is a technology-enthusiast, social media expert and all around CHIC GEEK! Aside from being the co-founder and Digital Immigration Officer of SynapseConnecting and Synapse 3Di, a technology and social engagement company, she is an international speaker, author of several books including Getting' Geeky with Twitter, and was the technical editor on the latest Complete Idiots Guide to Social Media! Gina also hosts the popular and fun tech shows, GETTIN' GEEKY, and SCHRECK TECK, where she helps people use today's technology to build business and engage communities. Gina was ranked as one of the top 50 women influencers on-line in FastCompany's Influence project.

Alice Heiman
www.aliceheiman.com

Informative, compelling, experienced and smart! Alice Heiman motivates her clients and makes a profound difference in the way they approach sales and their business.

A nationally recognized sales expert she has a proven record of leading and inspiring sales teams and is a catalyst for getting a business to the next level. Sales rep or business owner, her sales training will get them selling comfortably and successfully.

TIffany Denson
www.tlish.com

Owner of T. Lish Dressings, Marinades, & Sauces. Tiffany knows a thing or two about what it takes to launch a business! Tiffany created their business after the economic downturn and now you can find her product in stores and restaurants all over the country.

About The Author

Tammy is a broadly experienced marketing consultant, business strategist, and an entrepreneur mentor who has had the opportunity to consult with companies all over the globe.

She is an expert at identifying new ways to leverage the Internet for marketing gain.

Recently, Tammy re-launched her company under a different name, Perfect Marketing Equation.com.

In this new role she teaches entrepreneurs marketing tactics to grow their business by leveraging the Internet. In addition she consults with small businesses on their marketing strategies. She also designed a proprietary step-by-step system that teaches an entrepreneur all the fundamentals of marketing. The system takes the entrepreneur through a series of exercises and the end result is their own personal marketing plan that they will operate in everyday to take their business to the next level.

"It is truly the calling of my heart to help entrepreneurs navigate the craziness of the marketing world. I want to help them to do things the right way. I want their business to prosper and grow. Admittedly, it is an addiction and my passion to be a part of that process. I can't stand the thought of someone feeling alone and scared the way I have in the past. I want you to know you are not alone and it is okay to be afraid. You are incredibly courageous for what you are aspiring to do and you deserve to be successful. If you feel lost and alone please contact me! I will tell you myself!"

Connect with Tammy –

I would love to hear from you! Please contact me and let me know what you thought about my book!

If you are an entrepreneur that is struggling with taking your business to the next level I've been there! I have affordable mentoring programs that are structured to put you on the right path fast! *Don't do what I did!* Don't waste time spinning your wheels, being lost, and choosing the hardest path. Those choices cost money, time, and delay your success. Instead reach out to someone who has been there and can hold the flashlight for you. Mistakes are very expensive! More expensive than what a mentor is going cost.

I'm also interested in speaking engagements and will travel internationally. Please send me an email and tell me about your event.

The Web: www.perfectmarketingequation.com

Facebook: www.facebook.com/tammyhawkbridges

Twitter: www.twitter.com/thawkbridges

Email: tammy@perfectmarketingequation.com